African American Poetry

GLOBE BOOK COMPANY
A Division of Simon & Schuster
Englewood Cliffs, New Jersey

Photographic Interpretations Made by the Following Students:

Anton Cobb, 3, 49, 57, 61, 75, 77

Sidney Cutts, 4, 65

Alicia Garcia, 7

Jessica Forsyth, 11, 33, 45, 73

Jesse Wright, 13, 41

Eve Marsan, 15, 36, 82

Jane Joseph, 17

John Delgado, 18

Nikki Gilbert, 21

Michelle Pitts, 22

Kesha Moye, 26

Narda Brissett, 34

Danielle Hollomon, 38

Adam Kestin, 68

Dorothy Thomas, 71

Print acknowledgments can be found on pages 119 and 120.

Executive Editor: Virginia Seeley
Project Editor: Karen Hill
Art Director: Nancy Sharkey
Cover Design: Joan Jacobus
Production Manager: Winston Sukhnanand
Desktop Specialist: Danielle Hollomon
Marketing Manager: Elmer Ildefonso
Photo Research: Jenifer Hixson

Cover Photo: Anton Cobb

Printed in the United States of America.
10 9 8 7 6

ISBN 0–835–90533–0

 Globe Book Company
A Division of Simon & Schuster
Paramus, New Jersey

CONTENTS

UNIT FOUR

Bringing About Change: A Call for Revolution 37

UNIT FIVE

Portraits of Heroes 51

The Fullness of Life 72

ABOUT THE BOOK

This book of poetry is for you, the young adult of today. It is designed to help you appreciate poetry, and at the same time, bring you closer to the experiences of African Americans in this country. The book features the poetry of some of the best-known poets of the 19th and 20th centuries. It includes works by the forerunners of modern poetry, James Weldon Johnson and Paul Laurence Dunbar. It presents poets of the Harlem Renaissance such as Langston Hughes and Georgia Douglas Johnson. It takes you beyond the Renaissance and up to the present with contemporary poets such as Gwendolyn Brooks, Nikki Giovanni, and Amiri Baraka. You will be introduced to the rich world of African American culture through the poetry in this book. Allow the poetry to make you a part of this world.

ABOUT THE THEMES

You will notice that the poetry in this book is arranged according to themes. This organization is intended to capture the broad array of African American experiences throughout U.S. history. The themes reflect the joys and pains of African American life. They present the voices of people who have seen suffering, have felt anger, but most of all, have experienced pride, joy, and love. The themes show what is unique about being an African American; at the same time, they present images that are surprisingly similar regardless of culture. As you read the poems, try to recognize the unique as well as the universal elements within the themes.

THE POETRY AND YOU

Through the poetry in this book, you will experience the struggles that African Americans have faced. You will read about the oppression of slavery as well as the ever-present concerns of today, such as holding down a job or paying the rent on time. You will also become acquainted with the triumphs of the African American spirit. You will see that no obstacle is insurmountable and that no stumbling block is immovable. You will see that strength and persistence, tempered with love and laughter, are vital parts of the African American tradition.

These poems present both the positive and the negative; the good feelings and the bad. You will discover that both are there in the African American community. At the same time, you will discover that both are within you.

You will come to understand that these poems are about you—because not only do they relate to the African American experience, but to the experiences of all people. After reading Frank Horne's "To James," you will feel the same thrill of accomplishment felt after a "race well run." After reading Langston Hughes's "My People," you will experience the same pride in your heritage as the poet feels in his. After reading Desirée Barnwell's "Will the Real Black People Please Stand," you will experience the same anger that anyone would feel who believes that real issues are being overlooked in favor of trivial matters. These poems are about you and your world, and through the magical words and musical phrases of these poets, you will come to know yourself.

ABOUT THE PHOTOGRAPHS

The photographs used to illustrate this book were all taken by students. Globe went to several high schools in the northern New Jersey area to find photography students who might be interested in taking photographs for the book. Just as imagined, we found students who were more than interested. They were extremely excited about the project.

Each student was given a group of poems to illustrate. They read the poems, discussed them, then set out to shoot their interpretations. The students went to places where they have spent their lives: their homes, backyards, parks, streets, and, of course, school. They went out trying to capture the emotions and moods of the poems. They took what others might consider commonplace, and with their cameras, captured what they believed the poets and the poems were trying to say.

As the last photos were completed, we, the editors at Globe, and the students felt a great sense of accomplishment. The students felt pride in their creations, and we were awed by the creative talent of these young people. The whole experience was a great adventure and a learning experience for everyone involved!

SURVIVAL: MANY STRUGGLES MANY TRIUMPHS

Harlem Hopscotch

MAYA ANGELOU

One foot down, then hop! It's hot.
    Good things for the ones that's got.
Another jump, now to the left.
    Everybody for hisself.

In the air, now both feet down.
    Since you black, don't stick around.

Food is gone, the rent is due.
    Curse and cry and then jump two.

All the people out of work.
    Hold for three, then twist and jerk.
Cross the line, they count you out.
    That's what hopping's all about.

Both feet flat, the game is done.
They think I lost. I think I won.

Old Black Men

GEORGIA DOUGLAS JOHNSON

They have dreamed as young men dream
Of glory, love and power;
They have hoped as youth will hope
Of life's sun-minted hour.

They have seen as others saw
Their bubbles burst in air,
And they have learned to live it down
As though they did not care.

Midway

I've come this far to freedom and I won't turn back.
I'm climbing to the highway from my old dirt track.
   I'm coming and I'm going
   And I'm stretching and I'm growing
And I'll reap what I've been sowing or my skin's not black.

I've prayed and slaved and waited and I've sung my song.
You've bled me and you've starved me but I've still grown
   strong.
   You've lashed me and you've treed me
   And you've everything but freed me,
But in time you'll know you need me and it won't be long.

I've seen the daylight breaking high above the bough.
I've found my destination and I've made my vow;
   So whether you abhor me
   Or deride me or ignore me,
Mighty mountains loom before me and I won't stop now.

Love

Who is justice? I would like to know.
Whosoever she is, I could love her so;
I could love her, though my race
So seldom looks upon her face.

Sympathy

PAUL LAURENCE DUNBAR

I know what the caged bird feels, alas!
When the sun is bright on the upland slopes;
When the wind stirs soft through the springing
    grass,
And the river flows like a stream of glass;
When the first bird sings and the first bud opes,
And the faint perfume from its chalice steals—
I know what the caged bird feels!

I know why the caged bird beats his wing
Till its blood is red on the cruel bars;
For he must fly back to his perch and cling
When he fain would be on the bough a-swing;
And a pain still throbs in the old, old scars
And they pulse again with a keener sting—
I know why he beats his wing!

I know why the caged bird sings, ah me,
When his wing is bruised and his bosom sore,—
When he beats his bars and would be free;
It is not a carol of joy or glee,
But a prayer that he sends from his heart's
    deep core,
But a plea, that upward to Heaven he flings—
I know why the caged bird sings.

Wise 1

AMIRI BARAKA

If you ever find
yourself, some where
lost and surrounded
by enemies
who wont let you
speak in your own language
who destroy your statues
& instruments, who ban
your omm bomm ba boom
then you are in trouble
deep trouble
they ban your
oom boom ba boom
you in deep deep
trouble

humph!

probably take you several hundred years
to get
out!

To the Oppressors

PAULI MURRAY

Now you are strong
And we are but grapes aching with ripeness.
Crush us!
Squeeze from us all the brave life
Contained in these full skins.
But ours is a subtle strength
Potent with centuries of yearning,
Of being kegged and shut away
In dark forgotten places.

We shall endure
To steal your senses
In that lonely twilight
Of your winter's grief.

The Emancipation of George-Hector

(a colored turtle)

MARI E. EVANS

George-Hector
. . . is
spoiled.
formerly he stayed
well up in his
shell . . . but now
he hangs arms and legs
sprawlingly
in a most languorous fashion . . .
head rared back
to
be
admired.

he didn't use to
talk . . .
but
he does now.

Obstacles

LAYDING KALIBA

in light of the darkness
that prevails
what manner of flame have
you set to torch my life?
what new weight will you
add to my burden?
you have taken my laughter,
ridiculed my ambitions and
denounced my manhood.
in light of the darkness
that prevails,
what more can you do?

Still
I Rise

MAYA ANGELOU

You may write me down in history
With your bitter, twisted lies,
You may trod me in the very dirt
But still, like dust, I'll rise.

Does my sassiness upset you?
Why are you beset with gloom?
'Cause I walk like I've got oil wells
Pumping in my living room.

Just like moons and like suns,
With the certainty of tides,
Just like hopes springing high,
Still I'll rise.

Did you want to see me broken?
Bowed head and lowered eyes?
Shoulders falling down like teardrops,
Weakened by my soulful cries.

Does my haughtiness offend you?
Don't you take it awful hard
'Cause I laugh like I've got gold mines
Diggin' in my own back yard.

You may shoot me with your words,
You may cut me with your eyes,
You may kill me with your hatefulness,
But still, like air, I'll rise.

Out of the huts of history's shame
I rise
Up from a past that's rooted in pain
I rise
I'm a black ocean, leaping and wide,
Welling and swelling I bear in the tide.

Leaving behind nights of terror and fear
I rise
Into a daybreak that's wondrously clear
I rise
Bringing the gifts that my ancestors gave,
I am the dream and the hope of the slave.
I rise
I rise
I rise.

To James

FRANK HORNE

Do you remember
How you won
That last race . . . ?
How you flung your body
At the start . . .
How your spikes
Ripped the cinders
In the stretch . . .
How you catapulted
Through the tape . . .
Do you remember . . . ?
Don't you think
I lurched with you
Out of those starting holes . . . ?
Don't you think
My sinews tightened
At those first
Few strides . . .
And when you flew into the stretch
Was not all my thrill
Of a thousand races
In your blood . . . ?
At your final drive
Through the finish line
Did not my shout
Tell of the
Triumphant ecstasy
Of victory . . . ?

Live
As I have taught you
To run, Boy—
It's a short dash
Dig your starting holes
Deep and firm
Lurch out of them
Into the straightaway
With all the power
That is in you
Look straight ahead
To the finish line
Think only of the goal
Run straight
Run high
Run hard
Save nothing
And finish
With an ecstatic burst
That carries you
Hurtling
Through the tape
To victory.

EXPRESSIONS
OF
HOPE

the lesson of the falling leaves

LUCILLE CLIFTON

the leaves believe
such letting go is love
such love is faith
such faith is grace
such grace is god
i agree with the leaves

The Still Voice of Harlem

CONRAD KENT RIVERS

Come to me broken dreams and all
    bring me the glory of fruitless souls,
I shall find a place for them in my gardens.

Weep not for the golden sun of California,
    think not of the fertile soil of Alabama . . .
nor your father's eyes, your mother's body
    twisted by the washing board.

I am the hope of your unborn,
    truly, when there is no more of me . . .
there shall be no more of you . . . .

Speech to the Young/ Speech to the Progress-Toward

GWENDOLYN BROOKS

Say to them,
say to the down-keepers,
the sun-slappers,
the self-soilers,
the harmony-hushers,
"Even if you are not ready for day
it cannot always be night."
You will be right.
For that is the hard home-run.

Live not for battles won.
Live not for the-end-of-the-song.
Live in the along.

A Note of Humility

ARNA BONTEMPS

When all our hopes are sown on stony ground,
And we have yielded up the thought of gain,
Long after our last songs have lost their sound,
We may come back, we may come back again.

When thorns have choked the last green thing we loved,
And we have said all there is to say,
When love that moved us once leaves us unmoved,
Then men like us may come to have a day.

For it will be with us as with the bee,
The meager ant, the sea-gull and the loon;
We may come back to triumph mournfully
An hour or two, but it will not be soon.

Encouragement II

JOHN HENRIK CLARKE

Beyond the dark horizon,
Beyond the mass of glum,
If we can see a little hope
We can see the sun.
If we can mend our broken hearts
Hugging courage from despair,
Then we can grasp a brave new start,
And fight our way to anywhere.
We've suffered from the lack of might,
Yet we have survived the darkest day;
Now all we need is a little light
And we will find our way.

Dreams

LANGSTON HUGHES

Hold fast to dreams
For if dreams die
Life is a broken-winged bird
That cannot fly.

Hold fast to dreams
For when dreams go
Life is a barren field
Frozen with snow.

from *Dark Testament*

PAULI MURRAY

#8

Hope is a crushed stalk
Between clenched fingers.
Hope is a bird's wing
Broken by a stone.
Hope is a word in a tuneless ditty—
A word whispered with the wind,
A dream of forty acres and a mule,
A cabin of one's own and a moment to rest,
A name and place for one's children
And children's children at last . . .
Hope is a song in a weary throat.

> *Give me a song of hope*
> *And a world where I can sing it.*
> *Give me a song of faith*
> *And a people to believe in it.*
> *Give me a song of kindliness*
> *And a country where I can live it.*
> *Give me a song of hope and love*
> *And a brown girl's heart to hear it.*

23

A LEGACY OF PRIDE AND STRENGTH

Lift Ev'ry Voice and Sing

JAMES WELDON JOHNSON

Lift ev'ry voice and sing
Till earth and heaven ring,
Ring with the harmonies of Liberty;
Let our rejoicing rise
High as the listening skies,
Let it resound loud as the rolling sea.
Sing a song full of the faith that the dark past has
    taught us,
Sing a song full of the hope that the present has
    brought us,
Facing the rising sun of our new day begun
Let us march on till victory is won.

Stony the road we trod,
Bitter the chastening rod,
Felt in the days when hope unborn had died;
Yet with a steady beat,
Have not our weary feet
Come to the place for which our fathers sighed?
We have come over a way that with tears has
    been watered,
We have come, treading our path through the
    blood of the slaughtered,
Out from the gloomy past,

Till now we stand at last
Where the white gleam of our bright star is cast.
God of our weary years,
God of our silent tears,
Thou who has brought us thus far on the way;
Thou who has by Thy might
Led us into the light,
Keep us forever in the path, we pray.
Lest our feet stray from the places, our God,
    where we met Thee,
Lest, our hearts drunk with the wine of the
    world, we forget Thee;
Shadowed beneath Thy hand,
May we forever stand.
True to our God,
True to our native land.

Lineage

MARGARET WALKER

My grandmothers were strong.
They followed plows and bent to toil.
They moved through fields sowing seed.
They touched earth and grain grew.
They were full of sturdiness and singing.
My grandmothers were strong.

My grandmothers are full of memories.
Smelling of soap and onions and wet clay.
With veins rolling roughly over quick hands.
They have many cleans words to say.
My grandmothers were strong.
Why am I not as they?

My People

LANGSTON HUGHES

The night is beautiful,
So the faces of my people.

The stars are beautiful,
So the eyes of my people.

Beautiful, also, is the sun.
Beautiful, also, are the souls of my people.

Science . . .

GORDON NELSON

Science
   tells you
      Black is the
         absence of light

but
  your soul
     tells you Black
        is the light of the
          world.

What Color Is Black

BARBARA MAHONE

black is the color of
my little brother's mind
the grey streaks
in my mother's hair
black is the color of
my yellow cousin's smile
the scars upon my
neighbor's wrinkled face.
the color of
the blood we lose
the color of our eyes
is black.
our love of self
of others
brothers sisters
people of a thousand
shades of black
all one.
black is the color of
the feeling that we share
the love we must express
the color of our strength
is black.

We are . . .

HARDY CROSSLIN

right now that seems the most important thing
    to say
And it may seem bold to speak of tomorrow
    to people who have not been promised today

But we shall prevail because
We are

And we shall grow stronger until we know
    that efforts to stop us are foolish

Death cannot stop us

Even our own frailties will not stop us

On a mission for Truth and Justice

nothing can stop us

Growing stronger
And knowing more

We shall prevail,
We are

What Shall I Tell My Children Who Are Black

MARGARET BURROUGHS

What shall I tell my children who are black
Of what it means to be a captive in this dark skin
What shall I tell my dear ones, fruit of my womb,
Of how beautiful they are when everywhere they turn
They are faced with abhorrence of everything that is black.
Villains are black with black hearts.
A black cow gives no milk. A black hen lays no eggs.
Bad news comes bordered in black, black is evil
And evil is black and devil's food is black . . . .

What shall I tell my dear ones raised in a white world
A place where white has been made to represent
All that is good and pure and fine and decent.
Where clouds are white, and dolls, and heaven
Surely is a white, white place with angels
Robed in white, and cotton candy and ice cream
and milk and ruffled Sunday dresses
And dream houses and long sleek cadillacs
And angel's food is white . . . . all, all . . . white.

What can I say therefore, when my child
Comes home in tears because a playmate
Has called him black, big lipped, flatnosed
and nappy headed? What will he think
When I dry his tears and whisper "Yes, that's true.
But no less beautiful and dear."

How shall I lift up his head, get him to square
His shoulders, look his adversaries in the eye
Confident of the knowledge of his worth,
Serene under his sable skin and proud of his own beauty?
What can I do to give him strength
That he may come through life's adversities
As a whole human being unwarped and human in a world
Of biased laws and inhuman practices, that he might Survive.
And survive he must! For who knows? Perhaps this black
child
here bears the genius to discover the cure for . . . Cancer
Or to chart the course for exploration of the universe.
So, he must survive for the good of all humanity,
He must and will survive.
I have drunk deeply of late from the fountain
Of my black culture, sat at the knee and learned
From Mother Africa, discovered the truth of my heritage,
The truth, so often obscured and omitted.
And I find I have much to say to my black children

I will lift up their heads in proud blackness
With the story of their fathers and their fathers
Fathers. And I shall take them into a way back time
of Kings and Queens who ruled the Nile,
And measured the stars and discovered the
Laws of mathematics. Upon whose backs have been built
The wealth of continents. I will tell him
This and more. And his heritage shall be his weapon
And his armor; will make him strong enough to win
Any battle he may face. And since this story is
Often obscured, I must sacrifice to find it
For my children, even as I sacrifice to feed,

Clothe and shelter them. So this I will do for them
If I love them. None will do it for me.
I must find the truth of heritage for myself
And pass it on to them. In years to come I believe
Because I have armed them with the truth, my children
And their children's children will venerate me.
For it is the truth that will make us free!

from

African Poems

HAKI R. MADHUBUTI

WE'RE an Africanpeople
hard-softness burning black.
the earth's magic color our veins.
an Africanpeople are we;
burning blacker, softly, softer.

Women

ALICE WALKER

They were women then
My mama's generation
Husky of voice—Stout of
Step
With fists as well as
Hands
How they battered down
Doors
And ironed
Starched white
Shirts
How they led
Armies
Headragged Generals
Across mined
Fields
Booby-trapped
Ditches
To discover books
Desks
A place for us
How they knew what we
Must know
Without knowing a page
Of it
Themselves.

The Nature of this Flower Is to Bloom

ALICE WALKER

Rebellious. Living.
Against the Elemental Crush.
A Song of Color
Blooming
For Deserving Eyes.
Blooming Gloriously
For its Self.

Revolutionary Petunia.

BRINGING ABOUT CHANGE: A CALL FOR REVOLUTION

SOS

AMIRI BARAKA

Calling black people
Calling all black people, man woman child
Wherever you are, calling you, urgent, come in
Black People, come in, wherever you are, urgent, calling
you, calling all black people
calling all black people, come in, black people, come on in.

blk / rhetoric

SONIA SANCHEZ

who's gonna make all
that beautiful blk / rhetoric
mean something.
                              like
i mean
      who's gonna take
the words
      black / is / beautiful
and make more of it
than blk / capitalism.
                        u dig?
        i mean
                    like who's gonna
take all the young / long / haired
natural / brothers and sisters
and let them
                  grow till
                                    all that is
impt is them
                  selves
                        moving in straight /
revolutionary / lines
                        toward the enemy
(and we know who that is)
                        like. man.
who's gonna give our young
blk / people new heroes
like.this.   is an SOS
        me. calling . . . .
                                    calling . . . .
                                    some/one

        pleasereplysoon.

Will the Real Black People Please Stand

DESIRÉE A. BARNWELL

Will the real black people please stand:
Whose forefathers worked this land together,
Whose heritage is undated,
Whose pride remains uplifted;
Undaunted by the white man's statistics,
Pushed forward by initiative,
Unstilled by useless chatter.

Is this us:
Whose cooperation we dare not trust,
Irresponsible to past assignments,
Content to beat around the bush?
Stand up, black people . . .
Dressed in polka-dot shirts and striped ties,
Flowered, and possessed by them.
Is this really us?

Will the real black people please stand:
Those fearless of the unconventional.
Moved towards their own blackness,
Prone to influence and set trends,
Schooled in their times and folkways,
Dedicated to worthwhile endeavors,
Attentive to meaningful expression.

Is this us:
Uncommitted to work, driven to pleasure,
Preoccupied with semantics,
Hung up on ego projection,
Fooled by long talkers who say nothing,
Harassed by uncontrolled belligerence,
Cynical to the point of madness.
Is this really us?

Will the real black people please ACT.

Blessed Are Those Who Struggle

SULIAMAN EL HADI

Blessed are those who struggle
Oppression is worse than the grave
Better to die for a noble cause
than to live and die a slave

Blessed are those who courted death
Who offered their lives to give
Who dared to rebel, rather than serve
to die so that we might live

Blessed are those who took up arms
and dared to face our foes
Nat Turner,* Vesey,* Gabriel,* Cinque*
To mention a few names we know

Blessed are the memories of those who were there
at the Harper's Ferry Raid*
Strong were their hearts, noble their cause
and great was the price they paid

Blessed are the voices of those who stood up
and cried out, *Let us be free!*
Douglass* and Garvey* and Sojourner Truth*
Du Bois* and Drew Ali*

Blessed are the giants that we have loved
and lost to the bullet's sting
like Malcolm* and Medgar* and the Panthers* who fell
and Martin Luther King*

*These terms are defined in the glossary.

And blessed are the bodies of those who were hung
from the limbs of the sycamore tree
Who found end to their hope at the end of a rope
'cause they dared to attempt to be free

Up through the years we've continued this fight
our liberty to attain
And though we have faced insurmountable odds
yet the will to resist remains

Blessed are the spirits of those who have died
in the prisons all over this land
who committed one sin, they stood up like men
and got iced for just being a man

Blessed all you who will join with us now
in this struggle of life and death
so that freedom and peace will be more than a word
to the offspring that we have left.

Revolutionary Poets

JEAN A. PARRISH

revolutionary poets
    revolutionary feelers
      revolutionary movers
runnin down their
            revolutionary thought & feelin
to a potentially revolutionary people
and too few of them realize
that they
    along with the people
are only revolutionaries in the makin
that none of us
      have yet become
         true revolutionaries
we rap down our
      thoughts & feelins
about when the revolution comes
in hopes that the people
         the potential revolutionaries
will develop thoughts & feelins
       and move
towards the revolution
and join us
    in the process
      of becomin
revolutionaries
    we/us

the
    revolutionary poets
        feelers
            movers
    the revolutionary
            becomers.

Nation

CHARLIE COBB

Our hands have clenched hammers, hoes, and hope
Our backs have broken ground

around
the world

Our cries have crashed through terror
torn nights

Our bodies burnt
     the earth a bitter black

To rise

in
anger.

And I suppose
it
     will come
someday.

this thing
this black I am
that has to battle now

to
be

We will not have to say

someday,

nor fight
for what we are.

We! will be

simply
be,

We.
My children

or
    my
        children's
children

will know

We
    (are of roots
long, strong,
roots) which
grew into the world!

We!
the tree
seeds
we
spread
take root
grow
and my children shall know.
(meanwhile I) Search
for words:

Nation
Strength
People
    (now)

The Revolution Will Not Be Televised

GIL SCOTT-HERON

The revolution will not be televised.
The revolution will not be brought to you by Xerox* in four
    parts without commercial interruption.
The revolution will not show you pictures of Nixon*
    blowing a bugle and leading the charge by John
Mitchell,* General Abrams,* and Spiro Agnew,*
to eat hog mauls confiscated from a Harlem sanctuary.
The revolution will not be televised.

The revolution will not be brought to you
    by the Schaefer Award Theatre,*
and will not star Natalie Wood* as Steve McQueen*
or Bullwinkle* as Julia*.

The revolution will not give your mouth sex appeal.
The revolution will not get rid of the nubs.
The revolution will not make you look five pounds thinner
    because the revolution will not be televised, brother.

There will be no pictures of you and Willie Mays*
    pushing that shopping cart down the block on the
dead run,
or trying to slide that color TV into a stolen ambulance.
NBC will not be able to predict the winner at 8:32
    on reports from 29 districts.
The revolution will not be televised.

*These terms are defined in the glossary.

There will be no pictures of pigs shooting down brothers
 on the instant replay.
There will be no pictures of pigs shooting down brothers
 on the instant replay.

There will be no pictures of Whitney Young* being run out of
 Harlem on a rail, with a brand new process.
There will be no slow motion or still lifes of Roy Wilkins*
 strolling through Watts* in a red, black, and green
liberation jumpsuit that he has been saving
 for just the proper occasion.

*These terms are defined in the glossary.

"Green Acres,"* "Beverly Hillbillies,"* and "Hooterville
　　Junction"* will no longer be so damned relevant,
and women will not care if Dick finally got down with Jane
　　on "Search for Tomorrow"*
because black people will be in the street looking for a
　　brighter day.
The revolution will not be televised.

There will be no highlights on the 11 o'clock news,
　　and no pictures of Harry R.,* women liberationists,
and Jackie Onassis* blowing her nose.

The theme song will not be written by Jim Webb* or
　　Francis Scott Key*
nor sung by Glen Campbell,* Tom Jones,* Johnny Cash,*
　　Englebert Humperdinck,* or the Rare Earth.*
The revolution will not be televised.

The revolution will not be right back after a message
　　about a white tornado, white lightning, or white people.
You will not have to worry about a drum in your bedroom,
　　the tiger in your tank, or the giant in your toilet bowl.

The revolution will not go better with Coke.
The revolution will not fight germs that may cause bad
breath.
The revolution *will* put you in the driver's seat.

The revolution will not be televised.
. . . will not be televised.
. . . will not be televised.
. . . will not be televised.

The revolution will be no rerun, brothers.
The revolution will be *live!*

*These terms are defined in the glossary.

PORTRAITS
OF
HEROES

A Soliloquy to the Black Women of America

CHARLOTTE BROWN

Who Am I?
I'm a Black Woman!
Black like — Sojourner Truth . . . She bore thirteen babes
　　　　　　And not one of them was free;
　　　　　　She saw all of her thirteen children
　　　　　　Sold into slavery;
　　　　　　She preached for freedom and women's rights
　　　　　　Back in 1843;
　　　　　　She struggled hard and long
　　　　　　To change our destiny;
　　　　　　And She was Black—Like Me!

Black like — Harriet Tubman . . . A war nurse and a cook.
　　　　　　Who ran the freedom train;
　　　　　　She set a lot of people free.
　　　　　　Put her life on the line for liberty;
　　　　　　And She was Black—Like Me!

Black like — Edmonia Lewis . . . The first black woman
　　　　　　sculptor
　　　　　　In our land,
　　　　　　Her great works were "Hiawatha" and
　　　　　　"Forever Free";
　　　　　　Way back in 1870,
　　　　　　And She was Black—Like Me!

Black like — Geraldine McCullough—Who sculptured
Martin Luther King . . . Just right;
and Coretta Scott King, who
Carries on His fight!

Black like — The unassuming Gwendolyn Brooks,
Our poet of great note;
She won the coveted Pulitzer Prize
For the beautiful verse she wrote;
She brings enrichment to our lives
And She is Black—Like Me!

Black like — Lucy Terry . . . A Poet,
During the Colonial days;
And Phillis Wheatley . . . who published
her book
Of verse, while still a slave;
Maya Angelou and Nikki Giovanni . . .
We're proud
Of what they write;
They're known from sea to shining sea,
And They are Black—Like Me!

Black like— Lorraine Hansberry . . . Our great playwright,
Who died when much too young;
The fulfillment of her art
Had just begun;
No time for basking in the glory
Of her "Raisin in the Sun"!
Her great works we'll never see;
And She was Black—Like Me!

Black like — Our women in government
Skillfully balancing the scales of justice:
Jane Matilda Bolin . . . The First Black Woman
Judge in America;
Patricia Harris . . . The First Black Woman
appointed to a Presidential Cabinet;
Shirley Chisholm . . . Our First Black
Congresswoman;
Our first Congresswoman
From Texas . . . Barbara Jordan
From California . . . Yvonne Braithwaite Burke

From Illinois . . . Cardis Robertson Collins
While New York State Boasts
Of Constance Motley and Ersa Hines Poston;
Ida B. Wells Barnett . . . A Charter Member of
the NAACP
Fought for Anti-Lynching Laws . . . A freedom
fighter . . . She;

Sadie Alexander and Mary Church Terrell
Pressed forward for Civil Rights,
And Women's Rights . . . as well;
So many, many others of whom I stand, in awe,
They're working for us daily to broaden out
the law;
Working toward the day when we'll all be
truly free;
And all of them are Black—Black Like Me!

Black like — Marion Anderson . . . Whose rich contralto
voice was deemed
The Voice of the Century;
At the Metropolitan Opera House, She was
our first to sing;
Her songs, The Whole World's Legacy!
And She is Black—Like Me!

Dorothy Maynor's sweet classical Voice
Went right straight to our hearts!
She's working, still, to train our youth
At her "Harlem School of the Arts";
She's giving love and guidance,—Free!
And She is Black—Like Me!

Grace Bumbry and Mattiwilda Dobbs!
The great concert halls ring out their names
Elizabeth Greenfield and Leontyne Price!
All Prima Donnas of Opera Fame..

Of singers and actors, we claim quite a slew,
I pay homage here with these noted few:
Billie Holiday and Ella Fitzgerald!
Voices that long have thrilled the world;

Bessie Smith, Etta Moton and Ethel Waters!
Were some of our soulful singing daughters.

Josephine Baker, Pearl Bailey, Diahann
    Carroll and Lena Horne!
Put their vivid personalities into their songs.

Cicely Tyson, Diana Sands and Ruby Dee!
Everything actresses ought to be;

Hattie McDaniel in: "Gone With The Wind"
Copped the first Black "OSCAR" Win!

Florence Mills starred in "Shuffle Along"!
Some still remember her haunting song;

Mahalia Jackson in her own grand way,
Enriched our souls with her religious sway;

Pearl Primus and Kathryn Dunham!
Danced their way through every nation and
    kingdom;

They are yet hundreds more in this talent
    hunt spree,
And They're all Black—Like Me!

Black like — Madame C.J. Walker—Our First Black Millionaire!
She made us women more beautiful,
By dressing up our hair;
She bolstered up our confidence!
And She was Black—Like Me!

Black like — Maggie Walker of Richmond, Virginia;--who
Founded the huge St. Luke's Bank!
She was our First Bank President and Publisher of
    "The Herald"!
Still, she found time to build a home for destitute
    Black Girls;
She plunged ahead into the Economic Sea,
And She was Black—Like Me!

Our girls were banned from all of the college
societies,
So, Lucy Diggs Stowe, in 1908
Founded Alpha Kappa Alpha, It's grown to be
great!
Our First Sorority!

Susan McKinney Stewart . . . Our First Black
Woman Doctor
Practicing in New York City;

Marie Maynard Daly specialized
In Biological chemistry;

To better complete this medical verse
I mention our first black graduate nurse . . .
   Mary Elizabeth Mahoney!

Dr. Jeanne Noble, A Professor of Note!
"The Negro Woman's College Education"
The book that she wrote;
She taught my daughter at NYU
Of the intricacies of life and its values, too!
When men become Brothers, we'll all be free:
And She is Black--Like Me!

Althea Gibson . . . Our Tennis Star
At Forest Hills, Broke the Color Bar!

Black like — Wilma Rudolph . . . She's our Girl!
The greatest runner in all the world;
She won three gold medals in the Olympic
Game!
No other woman can make that claim;
Wilma stood tall and straight as a tree,
And She is Black—Like Me!

Black like — Rosa Parks . . . Who sat on a bus!
She held that seat for all of us;
The World cried out for Rosa's Right!
Our nation came to see the light;
Now, the choice of a seat . . . is Free!
And She is Black—Like Me!

Black like — Mary McLeod Bethune and Charlotte Hawkins
Brown!
Each raised a Black College in their chosen
town;

For ignorance had chained our people down,
They set a lot of young minds . . . Free!
And They were Black—Like Me!

There are millions of others,
The History Books do not recall;
The list of struggling Black Mothers,
The Mothers of us all!
They taught us to reach out!
They taught us to stand tall!
To be the most that we could be—
And They were Black—Like Me!

Who Am I?

I'm Somebody!

I'm a Black Woman!

Haiku

SONIA SANCHEZ

i have looked into
    my father's eyes and seen an
      african sunset.

I Know
A Lady

JOYCE CAROL THOMAS

I know a lady
A careful queen
She bows to no one
Her will is a
Fine thread of steel

Her blessing is a
Smile
Sinking its sails
Inside

Youth followed her around
The day she reached forty
Very few people knew—
Her face said twenty-two

Now somebody's embroidered silver
In her hair and sketched
A wrinkle here and there

I know a lady
A careful queen
She bows to no one

A Protest Poem for Rosa Parks

ABIODUN OYEWOLE

Every day for a long time now
I've been riding in the back
of the bus
sometimes I'm sitting
most times I'm standing
but if you look at my face
you can see my disgust
riding in the back of the bus
Now, today I'm real tired
just too tired to move
I done scrubbed floors
washed windows
I even polished ole Missy's shoes
the bus driver tells me
I got to give up my seat
'cause a white man wants it
and he just too good
to stand on his feet
Something in my gut
say I just don't give a damn
this seat I ain't givin' up
to hell with the white man
the white man he's waiting
for me to get up
and go to the back
I told him my feet hurt
and the back is already packed

You might as well
sound the alarm
and call the cops
this colored woman has gone mad
and she must be stopped
I didn't mind the handcuffs
or being in jail overnight
I still felt pretty strong
I guess I Knew I was right

Early that morning
revealed a brand-new day
A man named Martin Luther King
I was told was on his way
to see about me
and help Blacks get Equality
I felt good and started to sing
giving praise to the Lord
for Reverend Martin Luther King
when we first met
I'll never forget
the light in his eyes
he was our new Sunrise
to wake us up and win this Race
No matter how long
No matter how Blue
Martin was on a Mission
to make our dreams come true

We started the Montgomery Bus Boycott
and scared all the white folks in town
with Martin as our leader
we knew we would turn this thing around

we walked
used car pools
and worked together
with Victory in mind
having Faith that we'd win this battle
it was just a matter of time

The bus company went out of business
'cause WE didn't ride the bus
we discovered for the first time
the Power we had in US
Now when I look back
on that eventful day
I thank God and I pray
to never ever again
let anyone treat us like a slave

If We Forget

JA JAHANNES

If we forget
Who will keep the dream?
Who will celebrate?

Ancient portraits in black
Reaching back
Reaching forward to today
Timbuctu,* Zimbabwe*

If we forget
Who will keep the dream?
Who will celebrate?

If we forget
Who will care?
Who will share our pyramids,
store our past,
See our glory?
Share our story.
Who will celebrate
Malcolm* and Martin*
Whitney,* and Washington*
Lincoln* and Hampton*
Tuskegee*
Destinations, destiny?
Who will remember?

Who will remember?
Who will remember?
Who will remember me?
　　　If we forget
　　　Who will remember
　　　Shades of black

*These terms are defined in the glossary.

66

Reaching forward, reaching back
Ebony echoes growing strong
Singing songs
In the night
Richard Wright*
Slavery's sorrow
Slavery's pain
Freedom's struggle
Freedom's gain
Tubman's train*
Bethune* and Brooke*
Gwendolyn's* book
W.E.B.* and Owen's* too
Billie's* blues and Hughes's* blues
If we forget
Who will keep the dream?
Who will celebrate?
Who will remember
Robeson*
Muhammad* won
Burt's fun and Anderson*
Marshall's* Law
Pushkin* and Dumas?*
How far?
Can we go
If we forget?
If we forget
Who will remember?
Who will celebrate?

*These terms are defined in the glossary.

The Funeral of Martin Luther King, Jr.

NIKKI GIOVANNI

His headstone said
FREE AT LAST, FREE AT LAST
But death is a slave's freedom
We seek the freedom of free men
And the construction of a world
Where Martin Luther King could have lived and
    preached non-violence

For Malcolm, U.S.A.

JAMES EMANUEL

Thin, black javelin
Flying low.
Heads up!
Hear Malcolm go!

Cheekless tiger
On the prowl.
Breathlessly:
Hear Malcolm growl.

Lightning, lightning
Shot the sky.
Silently:
Did Malcolm die?

Brother, brother,
Hold my hand.
Malcolm was
My native land.

Alabama Poem

NIKKI GIOVANNI

If trees could talk
    wonder what they'd say
met an old man
    on the road late afternoon
    hat pulled over to shade
    his eyes
    jacket slumped over his shoulders
    told me "girl! my hands seen
    more than all
    them books they got
    at tuskegee"*
    smiled at me
    half waved his hand
    walked on down the dusty road
met an old woman
    with a corncob pipe
    sitting and rocking
    on a spring evening
    "sista" she called to me
    "let me tell you — my feet
    seen more than yo eyes
    ever gonna read"
    smiled at her and kept
    on moving
    gave it a thought and went
    back to the porch

*This term is defined in the glossary.

"i say gal" she called down
"you a student at the institute?
better come here and study
these feet
i'm gonna cut a bunion off
soons i gets up"
I looked at her
she laughed at me
if trees would talk
            wonder what they'd tell me

THE FULLNESS OF LIFE

Beca

NIKKI GIOVANNI

i wrote a poem for you because
you are
my little boy

i wrote a poem
for you because
you are
my darling daughter

and in this poem
i sang a song
that says
as time goes on
i am you
and you are me
and that's how life
goes on

Being Black in My Neighborhood

JA JAHANNES

Being Black in my neighborhood
Is a splendid thing
Like bright sunshine
And new clothes in Spring.

We got our own special ways
And our own special days,

Like Sunday morning.
Now that's a time
For colored boys and girls
To put on clothes as they say
And pose and strut,
Boys in their three piece suits,
Clean,
Know what I mean,
And girls so shiny
Hair greased back, with pretty curls
And bows and braids.
Ah, the whole neighborhood
Is laid.
Use to even be hats
And white patent leather pocketbooks
For handkerchiefs only.

Being Black in my neighborhood
Is a splendid thing,
Like singing in the Summer
On the corner
Under the moth encircled
Lamppost.

Oh, what joy it is
on my block
Being Black.

Those Winter Sundays

ROBERT HAYDEN

Sundays too my father got up early
and put his clothes on in the blueblack cold
then with cracked hands that ached
from labor in the weekday weather made
banked fires blaze. No one ever thanked him.

I'd wake and hear the cold splintering, breaking.
When the rooms were warm, he'd call,
and slowly I would rise and dress,
fearing the chronic angers of that house,

Speaking indifferently to him,
who had driven out the cold
and polished my good shoes as well.
What did I know, what did I know
of love's austere and lonely offices?

senses
of heritage

NTOZAKE SHANGE

my grandpa waz a doughboy from carolina
the other a garveyite* from lakewood
i got talked to abt the race and achievement
bout color and propriety/
nobody spoke to me about the moon

daddy talked abt music and mama bout christians
my sisters/we
always talked and talked
there waz never quiet
trees were status symbols

i've taken to fog/
the moon still surprisin me

*This term is defined in the glossary.

Variety in Black

DENISE SANDERS BROOKS

One day I heard someone say,
"All Black Folks look alike!"
That puzzled me
For as far as I could see,
We Black Folks represent variety.
Variety in style, interests and hue,
So numerous in examples,
I can name only a few.
Take Sister Stephanie
She is ebony.
Unique in style and deep in brown
Rich like the fertile soil of Africa,
Her aura so profound.
Stephanie—
Unlike you and unlike me,
Variety in Black.
There's Lydia
Childlike, energetic and determined,
Lydia will never grow old.
Unique in style and mahogany
She symbolizes the treasures of our young,
Laughing, enthusiastic, optimistic
Dancing to the pulse of the drum.
Lydia—
Unlike you and unlike me,
Variety in Black.

Mixed with the richness of coffee and the
sweetness of chocolate,
Mocha is what Jean seems.
Unique in style, pleasingly brown
Reaching for the sun; luminous, serene
An African queen.
Jean—
Unlike you and unlike me,
Variety in Black.

Now as you can see,
From this limited view of Black variety,
That in no way do I look like you
Or do you look like me.
Because Black folks come in all shapes and sizes,
With differences in style, interests and hue.
So the next time you hear someone say
"All Black Folks look alike,"
Dare them and defy them
to show you *two that do*!

one time
henry dreamed
the number

DOC LONG

"one time henry dreamed the number," she said
"but we didn't play it,
and do you know, that thing came out straight
3-67?
     yes it did!
we was both sick
for a whole week,
     could'a sure used
             the money then too.
that was back in hoover's* time
when folks was scufflin
to make ends meet.
i knock on wood though
             we've lived through it all.
last night after we ate
the last of the meat loaf and greens
and was watching television
henry asked me if i remembered that,
i told him yes,
     we laughed
     then went to bed
and kept each other warm."

*This term is defined in the glossary.

80

Our Promise

PHYLLIS BYNUM

Beautiful sister and handsome young brother
You live in a city unlike any other.

With millions of people who hurry about,
Going here, going there, trying to figure it out.

There are people who come here from far, far away
To see all the sights and especially Broadway.

You can see the Bronx Zoo, Brooklyn Bridge,
   and Twin Towers,
There are things in museums you can stare at
   for hours.

There are gardens and airports, the world's
   tallest steeple,
And foods from all nations to please all the people.

You are young, you are strong, you are able and
   smart,
You can make a big difference, give us all a fresh
   start.

We're depending on you to come up with solutions
For poverty, war, and a thousand pollutions.

We know you can do what you plan to achieve,
Go ahead, take a chance, you just have to
   believe.

You show promise to change all the ills of the past,
Make King's dream come true—to "Be Free At Last!"

You are treasures to fathers and mothers and teachers,
Get away from the corners, come down from the
    bleachers.

Go stand center field, stand tall and be proud,
Say, "I will be a winner!" and shout it out loud!

THE POEM
IN
REVIEW

SURVIVAL: MANY STRUGGLES MANY TRIUMPHS

Harlem Hopscotch (p. 2)

1. How do the ideas in this poem make you feel? Which words, phrases, or images in the poem help to bring about these feelings?

2. How do you think Angelou's childhood experiences as an African American girl are reflected in this poem?

3. How does the game of hopscotch help to reveal the poem's theme? How does the line "They think I lost. I think I won" link this poem's theme to the unit theme of survival?

Old Black Men (p. 4)

1. How did reading this poem make you feel? Which specific words or phrases made you feel this way?

2. What do you believe is Johnson's attitude toward these old black men?

3. What is the theme or message of this poem? How does the poem's theme reveal the African American experience?

Midway (p. 5)

1. How does this poem make you feel? How do the rhyme and the rhythm enhance this feeling?

2. In what ways does this poem reflect Madgett's perspective as an African American woman?

3. What is the theme of this poem?

Love   (p. 5)

1. Has reading this poem changed the way you think about justice? Explain your answer.
2. What does Clarke tell you about his attitude toward the condition of his people?
3. Briefly state what you believe to be the theme of this poem.

Sympathy   (p. 6)

1. What emotions does this poem awaken in you? Which phrases or images in the poem help to create these emotions?
2. What does this poem reveal about Dunbar's attitude as an African American?
3. Briefly state what you believe to be the poem's message. How does the image of the caged bird convey this message?

Wise 1   (p. 8)

1. What feelings were you left with after reading this poem? How does the repetition of words help to reinforce these feelings?
2. How does this poem reflect Baraka's attitude toward his African heritage and toward white culture?
3. What is the central idea of the poem?

To the Oppressors   (p. 9)

1. How do the ideas in this poem make you feel? How does the vivid language enhance these feelings?
2. How does Murray convey her pride in her African American heritage?
3. What is the central message of this poem?

The Emancipation of
George-Hector *(a colored turtle)* *(p. 10)*

1. What thoughts were you left with after reading this poem?
2. How does this poem reflect Evans's attitude toward her identity as an African American and as a woman?
3. Briefly discuss the theme of this poem. How does the image of the turtle reinforce the theme?

Obstacles *(p. 11)*

1. How does this poem make you feel? Which specific words or phrases reinforce these feelings?
2. What does Kaliba reveal about his attitude toward the obstacles he confronts?
3. Briefly state what you believe to be the theme of this poem.

Still I Rise *(p. 12)*

1. What emotions does the poem awaken in you? Jot down specific words or images that reinforce these emotions.
2. In what ways does this poem reflect Angelou's outlook as an African American and as a woman?
3. In one sentence, state what you believe to be the poet's message.

To James *(p. 14)*

1. Is the speaker's advice to James similar to any advice you have been given? Explain your answer.
2. What does Horne's enthusiasm for running suggest about the way he views life?
3. What is the theme of this poem? How does the race help to reveal the theme?

UNIT TWO

EXPRESSIONS OF HOPE

the lesson of the falling leaves (p. 17)

1. How do the ideas expressed in this poem relate to any experiences in your life?
2. What does the last line of this poem reveal about Clifton's attitude toward nature?
3. What is the theme of this poem? How is this theme an expression of hope?

The Still Voice of Harlem (p. 18)

1. What thoughts and emotions does this poem bring out in you?
2. What does Rivers reveal about his attitude toward his ancestors?
3. Briefly discuss the theme of this poem.

Speech to the Young/Speech to the Progress-Toward (p. 19)

1. Describe ways in which the poet's advice relates to your life.
2. What does this poem reveal about the way Brooks lives her life?
3. Briefly discuss the poet's message.

A Note of Humility (p. 20)

1. Describe the emotions this poem brought out in you. Which specific words and phrases reinforced these emotions?
2. What hope for the future does Bontemps reveal in the poem?
3. What is the message of the poem?

Encouragement II *(p. 21)*

1. How do the poem's ideas relate to experiences in your life?
2. What does Clarke tell you in the poem about the way he views his life?
3. What is the theme of this poem?

Dreams *(p. 22)*

1. What dreams of your own does this poem call to mind?
2. What does Hughes reveal in this poem about his attitude toward life?
3. Briefly discuss the theme of this poem. How does it relate to the unit theme of "expressions of hope"?

from *Dark Testament* *(p. 23)*

1. What thoughts were you left with after reading this poem?
2. How do Murray's hopes in this poem reflect her outlook as an African American?
3. What is the message of this poem?

UNIT THREE

A LEGACY OF PRIDE AND STRENGTH

Lift Ev'ry Voice and Sing *(p. 25)*

1. How did you feel while reading this poem? Which words, phrases, or images helped to bring about these emotions?
2. What does Johnson reveal about his attitude toward values such as faith, hope, and loyalty?
3. What do you believe is the central message of this poem?

Lineage *(p. 27)*

1. What memories of your ancestors does this poem bring about? How do they compare to the speaker's observations of her ancestors?
2. What does the last line of the poem suggest about Walker's sense of identity?
3. Briefly state what you believe to be the theme of this poem.

My People *(p. 28)*

1. How do the ideas expressed in this poem make you feel? How does the repetition of certain words enhance your feelings?
2. How does Hughes reveal his attitude toward his people?
3. What is this poem's theme?

Science . . . *(p. 28)*

1. How do you feel about the speaker's observations in this poem?
2. What does this poem reveal about the way Nelson views life?
3. How does the poem's theme relate to the unit theme of "pride and strength"?

What Color Is Black *(p. 29)*

1. What emotions does this poem bring about in you? Which words, phrases, or images reinforce these emotions?
2. What does this poem reveal about Mahone's attitude toward her people?
3. Briefly discuss the theme of this poem.

We are . . . *(p. 30)*

1. Has reading the poem changed the way you think about your own identity? Explain your answer.
2. What does Crosslin's optimism tell you about the way he views his life?

3. State what you believe to be the theme of this poem by completing its title, "We are . . . ."

What Shall I Tell My Children Who Are Black *(p. 31)*

1. How did reading this poem influence the way you think about your own identity?
2. How does Burroughs's knowledge of her heritage help her to overcome racial prejudice?
3. Discuss the theme of the poem by answering the question "What shall I tell my children who are . . . .?"

from African Poems *(p. 34)*

1. Has reading this poem influenced the way you think about your own culture? Explain your answer.
2. What is Madhubuti's attitude toward his people and his cultural heritage?
3. What is the poem's theme?

Women *(p. 35)*

1. What feelings were you left with after reading this poem?
2. What qualities about her mother's generation does Walker most admire?
3. What is the theme of this poem?

The Nature of this Flower Is to Bloom *(p. 36)*

1. What were your reactions to this poem? How do the ideas in it relate to an experience in your own life?
2. In this poem, Walker uses the imagery of a blooming flower to symbolize her people. What qualities does Walker recognize in her people?
3. Briefly discuss the theme of this poem. How does the title of the poem reflect the theme?

UNIT FOUR

BRINGING ABOUT CHANGE: A CALL FOR REVOLUTION

SOS *(p. 38)*

1. What feelings or thoughts were you left with after reading this poem?
2. Describe what you believe to be Baraka's attitude in this poem. How does his repeated use of the word "urgent" reflect this attitude?
3. "SOS" is a common call for help. How does the title "SOS" relate to the message of the poem?

blk/rhetoric *(p. 39)*

1. What questions were you left with after reading this poem?
2. Sanchez has said that "The Black writer/artist must reflect the times. Must be the technicians of the people. Must be the mind/changers." Discuss how in this poem Sanchez lives up to her own definition of a black writer as a technician of the people and a mind/changer.
3. Rhetoric is verbal communication—or talk—which can sometimes be lofty and insincere. How does the message of the poem relate to this definition?

Will the Real Black People Please Stand *(p. 40)*

1. What are your thoughts after reading this poem? Which specific words or phrases caused you to think as you do?
2. What do you believe is Barnwell's attitude toward her African American heritage?
3. Briefly discuss the message of the poem.

Blessed Are Those Who Struggle *(p. 42)*

1. How has reading this poem influenced the way you think about peace, rebellion, and freedom?

2. What does this poem reveal about the way El Hadi views life and death?

3. What is the theme of this poem?

Revolutionary Poets (p. 44)

1. What is your reaction to this poem?
2. How does Parrish, as a poet, view her role in the revolution?
3. What is the poet's message?

Nation (p. 46)

1. How did reading this poem influence the way you think about the struggles of your own people?
2. What does Cobb reveal about his hope for the future generations of African Americans?
3. How does the last stanza convey the poem's theme?

The Revolution Will Not Be Televised (p. 48)

1. How did reading this poem influence the way you think about the role of the television in society?
2. How does this poem reveal Scott-Heron's attitude towards white society? How does it reveal white society's attitude toward African Americans?
3. Briefly discuss the theme of this poem.

UNIT FIVE

PORTRAITS OF HEROES

A Soliloquy to the Black Women of America (p. 52)

1. Which famous figure(s) in this poem is (are) especially meaningful to you? Why?

2. How does this poem reflect Brown's pride in African American women?

3. Briefly discuss the theme of this poem.

Haiku *(p. 61)*

1. What emotions does this poem bring about in you?

2. How would you relate Sanchez's attitude toward her father to her attitude about her African heritage?

3. How does the poem's theme relate to the unit theme of "portraits of heroes"?

I Know a Lady *(p. 62)*

1. Does the lady described in this poem remind you of someone you know and admire? Explain your response.

2. Which qualities in this lady does Thomas admire?

3. Briefly discuss the theme of this poem. In what ways is this lady a hero?

A Protest Poem for Rosa Parks *(p. 63)*

1. How did reading this poem change or confirm the way you think about Rosa Parks and Martin Luther King, Jr.?

2. How does this poem express Oyewole's attitude toward his ancestors?

3. What is the message of this poem?

If We Forget *(p. 66)*

1. What feelings and memories does this poem awaken in you?

2. How does Jahannes reveal his pride in his cultural heritage?

3. How does the poem's theme relate to the unit theme of heroes?

The Funeral of Martin Luther King, Jr. *(p. 68)*

1. How did reading this poem affect the way you think about the life of Martin Luther King, Jr.?
2. What does this poem reveal about Giovanni's attitude about the treatment of African Americans in today's society?
3. Briefly discuss the theme of this poem.

For Malcolm, U.S.A. *(p. 69)*

1. How did reading this poem influence the way you think about Malcolm X?
2. How do the first two stanzas capture Emanuel's perception of Malcolm X?
3. What do you believe is the poet's message?

Alabama Poem *(p. 70)*

1. What does this poem make you feel about your own ancestors? Explain your answer.
2. How does Giovanni express her respect for her ancestors in this poem?
3. Briefly discuss the theme of this poem. In what ways are the old man and woman the poet's heroes?

UNIT SIX

THE FULLNESS OF LIFE

Because *(p. 73)*

1. What was your reaction to this poem?
2. In this poem, what does Giovanni tell you about her concept of family?
3. What do you believe is the poet's message?

Being Black in My Neighborhood (p. 74)

1. Which rituals and traditions of your cultural heritage does this poem call to mind?
2. What does this poem reveal about Jahannes's attitude toward his people?
3. Briefly discuss the message of the poem.

Those Winter Sundays (p. 76)

1. How did reading this poem change the way you think about your own parents?
2. Which of his father's qualities do you believe Hayden admires?
3. Briefly discuss the theme of the poem.

senses of heritage (p. 77)

1. What experiences of your own does this poem bring to mind?
2. What does Shange's childhood fascination with the moon suggest about the way she views life?
3. Briefly discuss the theme of this poem. How does the poem's theme relate to the unit theme of "the fullness of life"?

Variety in Black (p. 78)

1. How did reading this poem influence the way you think about the differences between you and your friends? Jot down some qualities that you possess that make you unique.
2. What does this poem suggest about the way Brooks views herself?
3. What is the poet's message?

one time henry dreamed the number (p. 80)

1. Does this poem influence the way you look at relationships? Explain your answer.

2. How does this poem reflect Long's optimistic outlook on life?
3. What is the theme of this poem? How does it relate to the unit theme of "the fullness of life"?

Our Promise *(p. 81)*

1. How would you respond if the poet spoke the lines of this poem to you personally?
2. What do you believe is Bynum's attitude toward the youth of today? Which lines from the poem cause you to believe as you do?
3. What do you believe is the theme of this poem? How does the title, "Our Promise," reflect this theme?

BIOGRAPHIES OF POETS

Maya Angelou (1928-) was born in St. Louis, Missouri. Angelou is the author of *Just Give Me A Cool Drink of Water 'fore I Diiie* (1971), *Oh Pray My Wings Are Going to Fit Me Well* (1975), and *And Still I Rise* (1976). She is also the author of four autobiographical works: *I know Why the Caged Bird Sing* (1970), *Gather Together In My Name* (1974), *Singin' and Swingin' and Gettin' Merry Like Christmas"* (1976) and *Heart of a Woman* (1981). Angelou is a playwright, stage and screen performer and activist. She has been awarded the 1992 Essence Awards and 1992 Langston Hughes Award from the City College of New York.

Amiri Baraka (formerly LeRoi Jones) (1934-) is a poet, teacher, activist, and griot-style storyteller. Baraka was born in Newark, New Jersey and was educated at Howard University and Rutgers University. His Muslim Bantu name means "blessed prince." Baraka is the author of thirteen books of poetry, twenty plays, six nonfiction books and two jazz operas. Baraka is the consummate African American revolutionary poet. Notable among his works are *Blues People* (1963), *Preface to a Twenty Volume Suicide Note* (1961), and *Confirmation* (1985). He has received the Obie Award (1964), Guggenheim Award (1965), a Doctor of Letters from Malcolm X College in Chicago, and the American Book Award. Currently, Baraka is Associate Professor of Africana Studies at SUNY in Stony Brook, New York.

Desirée A. Barnwell (also known as Mrs. Lawrence S. Cumberbatch) is a native of Guyana, South America. She is a graduate of Queens College in New York, with a degree in sociology. Her poem "Will the Real Black People Please Stand" was first published in *Night Comes Softly* (1970), a collection of African American women's poetry, edited by Nikki Giovanni.

Arna Bontemps (1902-1973) was a key figure during the Harlem Renaissance and was the author of over thirty books. Bontemps was born in Alexandria, Louisiana, and was educated at Pacific Union College and the University of Chicago. He was the Chief Librarian at Fisk University and curator of the James Weldon Johnson Memorial Collection at

Yale University. Bontemps's poetic works amounted to one book, *Personals*, published in 1964. Bontemps was the recipient of a Rosenwald Fellowship (1938) and a Guggenheim Fellowship (1965). He was a close friend and literary associate of Langston Hughes. He collaborated with Hughes on *The Poetry of the Negro* (1950) and *American Negro Poetry* (1963).

Denise Sanders Brooks (1953-) was born in Newark, New Jersey. She is a poet and writer who, along with her husband and two sons, makes her home in Linden, New Jersey. Brooks is a graduate of St. Peter's College in Jersey City, and has been a creative writer since grammar school. Much of her poetry is lyrical, and written to jazz rhythms. Her poetry has appeared in several New Jersey publications.

Gwendolyn Brooks (1917-) was the first African American woman to receive the Pulitzer Prize (1950) for her poetry collection *Annie Allen*. Brooks was born in Topeka, Kansas and currently lives in Chicago. She is the Poet Laureate of Illinois. Brooks is the author of many notable works, including *A Street in Bronzeville* (1945), *The Bean Eaters* (1960), *Aloneness* (1971), *The Tiger Who Wore White Gloves* (1974), and *Primer for Blacks* (1980). Brooks is known for her technical mastery of poetic forms as well as her directness and clarity in later works. Brooks was the "mother" of many of the young poets of the sixties and continues to influence and teach young poets and writers.

Charlotte Brown is a poet, writer, composer, and humanitarian. She is a graduate of Adelphi University. Brown is the author of two collections of poetry: *Feeling Black* and *Dark Ashes*. Brown's poetry has been produced on CBS-TV and performed in many settings. Brown is the mother of five and a grandmother of four.

Margaret Burroughs (1917-) is an artist, poet, teacher, and curator. Burroughs was born in St. Rose, Louisiana. She was educated at the Art Institute of Chicago, Esmerelda Art School and Columbia University. Burroughs is the founder of the DuSable Museum of African American History in Chicago. Burroughs has exhibited her art all over the world. She is the author of *Jasper the Drummin' Boy* (1970), *What Shall I Tell My Children* (1973), and *Africa, My Africa* (1970). She also holds an honorary doctorate of Honoris Causis from Lewis College.

Phyllis Bynum (1937-) was born in Richmond, Virginia, and now resides in New York City. Bynum is a graduate of Spelman College in Atlanta, Georgia and has done graduate studies in Early Childhood Education at New York University and City University of New York. Bynum is an educator with a special appreciation for language and literature. She frequently presents workshops dealing with topics in education—usually with generous servings of poetry. "Our Promise" is part of her first collection of poetry entitled *Refined Reflection*, published in 1989. Bynum's second collection, *She Said*, was published in 1992.

John Henrik Clarke (1915-)—elder, griot, and keeper of African history—was born in Alabama but grew up in Columbus, Georgia. He studied creative writing at Columbia University. Clarke is the author of *The Lives of Great African Chiefs*, and he has been the editor of the anthologies *Harlem USA*, *Freedomways Magazine*, *Negro History Bulletin*, and *The Harlem Quarterly*. Clarke is Professor Emeritus of African and World History at Hunter College. Most recently he published *African World Revolution: Africans at the Crossroads* (1992).

Lucille Clifton (1936-) was born in Depew, New York, and is the Poet Laureate of Maryland. Educated at Howard University and the State University at Fredonia, she has been nominated twice for the Pulitzer Prize and has been awarded the Juniper Prize from the University of Massachusetts Press. She is also the recipient of an Emmy Award and several NEA creative writing fellowships. Outstanding among her works are *Good Times* (1969), *Good News About the Earth* (1972), *An Ordinary Woman* (1974), *Two-Headed Woman* (1976), and *Good Woman: Poems and a Memoir 1969-1980*. She has also published several books of children's poetry and fiction. A mother of six, Clifton is presently the Distinguished Visiting Professor at St. Mary's College of Maryland. Her most recent book is *Quilting* (1992).

Charlie Cobb (1944-) is a poet and was a well-known field-secretary for SNCC (Student Non-Violent Coordinating Committee) in the 1960s. He attended Howard University but dropped out to become an activist in the Civil Rights Movement. He worked extensively to establish "Freedom Schools" throughout the South. He was a Foreign Affairs news reporter for National Public Radio and was the founder of Drum and Spear Press. His poetry collections include *Furrows* (1967) and *Everywhere is Ours* (1971).

Hardy Crosslin is a native of Daytona Beach, Florida. He studied philosophy at Morehouse College in Atlanta, Georgia. Later, the poet and novelist became a member of the famed John O. Killens writers workshop at Medgar Evers College in New York. Crosslin is currently at work on a novel about the Civil Rights Movement.

Paul Laurence Dunbar (1872-1906) was born in Dayton, Ohio. Dunbar was one of the most popular poets of his day and is widely anthologized throughout the world. Dunbar wrote poetry while in grade school and was the first black writer to make his living solely from his writing. His most well known works are found in *Oak and Ivory* (1893), *Lyrics of a Lowly Life* (1896) and *Lyrics of Sunshine and Shadow* (1905). Dunbar was known as a "dialect" poet. He suffered intense poverty and a host of illnesses throughout his short life. Before his premature death from tuberculosis, Dunbar also wrote four novels, four collections of short stories, librettos and musicals.

Suliaman El Hadi was a member of the Last Poets of the late 1960s, the group whose music has been called the original rap music. His poetry is born out of the struggle and protest activity of the late 1960s. He is the co-author of *The Last Poets, Vibes From the Scribes* (1992). He has also recorded his work on the albums *The Last Poets* (1970) and *This Is Madness* (1971).

James Emanuel (1921-) was born in Alliance, Nebraska. He participated in World War II and spent his early years in the army in the Pacific. Emanuel later studied at Howard University and Columbia University, where he received a doctorate degree in 1962. He introduced the first black poetry course at the City College of New York. His first book of poetry was *Treehouse* (1968), followed by *Panther Man* (1970) and *A Poets Mind* (1983). He also co-edited *Dark Symphony: Negro Literature in America*.

Mari E. Evans (1923-)—poet, writer, editor, musician, TV producer and director—was born in Toledo, Ohio. Evans, who started writing in the fourth grade, is known for her humorous touch. She is a graduate of Toledo University. Her first book of poetry was *Where Is All the Music?* Evans received critical acclaim for her book *I Am the Black Woman* (1970). She went on to write *JD* (1973) and *Rap Stories* (1974). Evans's poetry can be found in over 200 anthologies. She is a recipient of an NEA Award and a John Hay Whitney Fellow.

Nikki Giovanni (1943-) was born in Knoxville, Tennessee. Giovanni was the princess of African American poetry during the 1960s. She graduated from Fisk University and attended Columbia University. Giovanni is known for her black revolutionary verse as well as her verse for children. Her most popular works include: *Black Feeling, Black Talk, Black Judgement* (1968), *Re: Creation* (1970), *My House* (1972), and *Cotton Candy on a Rainy Day* (1978). Giovanni has been a professor at Queens College and Rutgers University. Giovanni was among the leading poets of the 1960s and is now a popular lecturer and contributor to scholarly and popular magazines. She now lives in Ohio with her son.

Robert E. Hayden (1913-1980) was born in Detroit, Michigan and was educated at Wayne State University. Hayden had a long literary career as a poet, professor, playwright and editor. He worked for the Federal Writers Project, researching local Negro history and folklore. He was the recipient of the Hopwood Awards (1938 and 1942) from the University of Michigan, a Rosenwald Fellow in 1947 and a Ford Foundation Grant in 1945. He was a Professor of English at Fisk University. Hayden is the author of *Heartshape in the Dust, Middle Passage, A Ballad of Remembrance*, and *Robert Hayden: Collected Poems* which won the grand prize in the First World Festival of Negro Arts held in Dakar, Senegal in 1962. He was also the recipient of the National Book Award and was an Academy of American Poets Fellow in 1977. Hayden was known for his well-crafted, emotionally mature poems which have a universal appeal.

Frank Horne (1899-1974) was born in Brooklyn, New York. Horne was an optometrist, an official with the United States Housing Authority, and was known as "race" man. He was first discovered when he was awarded the Crisis poetry prize in 1925 for *Letters Found Near a Suicide*. His most memorable works are *Letters Found Near a Suicide* and his collected works

Haverstraw. He is the uncle of Lena Horne. Horne's poetry is a mixture of satire and irony.

Langston Hughes (1902-1967) was considered the African American poetic genius of this century. Hughes was born in Joplin, Missouri. Hughes attended Columbia University for one year, but left school and signed on as a seaman on a cargo ship. Hughes later graduated from Lincoln University in 1929. Hughes first came to print with the *Weary Blues* (1926), which was quickly followed by *Fine Clothes to the Jew*. He was a prolific writer and translator who published over thirty books including: *Not Without Laughter* (1930), *One Way Ticket* (1949), *Montage of a Dream Deferred* (1951), *The Poetry of the Negro 1746-1949*, and *The Panther and the Lash* (1967). Hughes participated in the Negritude movement of the thirties. He became the recipient of such awards as the Harmon Gold Award in 1931, the Guggenheim Fellowship in 1935, and the Spingarn Medal in 1960. He was elected to the American Academy of Arts and Letters in 1961. Hughes made his American home in Harlem. He came to be known as the Poet Laureate of Harlem.

Ja Jahannes (1942-) is a poet, scholar, psychologist, playwright and ordained minister. He was educated at Lincoln University and the University of Delaware. He has traveled and taught in Africa, Asia and Latin America. Jahannes is the author of *Truthfeasting* (1990) and *Black Generation* (1989). He has been awarded the Atlantic Center for Art Fellowship and a Langston Hughes Cultural Arts Award.

Georgia Douglas Johnson (1886-1966) was a poet of the Harlem Renaissance whose work has been the subject of renewed interest in the 1990s. Johnson studied music at the Oberlin Conservatory in Ohio but opted to be a poet. She received an honorary doctorate in literature from the Atlanta University. Her most outstanding works are *The Heart of a Woman* (1918), *Bronze* (1922), *An Autumn Love Cycle* (1928), and *Share My World* (1962). Johnson combined a literary career with government work and kept a popular artists' salon in her Washington, D.C. home during the Harlem Renaissance.

James Weldon Johnson (1871-1938) was born in Jacksonville, Florida. He was a writer of exceptional talent and genius. Johnson made his living as a writer, poet, playwright and lawyer. He was the first African American in Florida to be admitted to the state bar. Notable among his many texts are *The Autobiography of an Ex-Colored Man* (1912) and *God's Trombones* (1927). Johnson served as the first Executive Secretary of the NAACP. He was Professor of Creative Literature at Fisk University and New York University and was awarded the Spingarn Award.

Layding Kaliba (1947-) was born in Harlem, New York. Kaliba is a poet and publisher of Single Action Productions. He is the author of *Still Outraged* (1979), *Up on the Down Side* (1982) and *The Moon Is My Witness* (1988). Kaliba is a self-taught, self-published poet whose inspiration came directly from the Black Arts Movement of the 1960s. He has been published in *Essence Magazine*, *Catalyst Magazine*, and *Black Books Bulletin*. He is also a founding member of Our Own Bookfair Artist Consortium.

Doc Long (1942-) is a native of Atlanta, Georgia. He is the author of *Black Love, Black Hope* (1970), and *Song for Nia* (1971). Long is a world traveler whose poetry can be found in many African American poetry anthologies.

Naomi Long Madgett (1923-), known for her lyrical poetry, is the author of *Songs to a Phantom Nightingale* (1941), *One and the Many* (1956), and *Star by Star* (1965). Madgett was born in Norfolk, Virginia and was educated at Wayne State University and Virginia State University. She has been awarded the Mott Fellow in English at Oakland University. Madgett was the Associate Professor of English at the University of Eastern Michigan and is also the Associate Editor of Lotus Press. Madgett recently edited *Adam of Ife: Black Women in Praise of Black Men*.

Haki Madhubuti (formerly Don L. Lee) (1942-) is a native of Little Rock, Arkansas, though he was raised in Detroit. Madhubuti graduated from the University of Illinois and the University of Iowa. Madhubuti is the publisher and editor of Third World Press in Chicago. He is also the director of the Institute of Positive Education. He is the author of *Think Black* (1967), *Black Pride* (1969), *Don't Cry, Scream* (1969), *We Walk the Way of the New World* (1970), and *Black Males: Obsolete, Single, and Dangerous?* (1991). Madhubuti formerly was writer-in-residence at Cornell University and Harvard University. He was a book reviewer for *Black World* during the sixties and compiled the journal *Dynamite Voices*. In recent years he has published *Black Books Bulletin* and continues to publish individual volumes of up-and-coming poets.

Barbara Mahone (1944-) was born in Chicago. She is a poet and mother currently living in Atlanta, Georgia. She was a member of the writers workshop of OBAC in Chicago. Mahone is the author of *Sugarfields* (1970).

Pauli Murray (1910-1985) was born in Baltimore, Maryland. Murray was considered a trailblazer and enjoyed a broad career as a poet, lawyer, professor, activist and priest. Murray graduated from Hunter College, Howard University, and Yale University. She was the first woman in America to be ordained as an Episcopal priest. Murray was also among the first Freedom Riders in the 1940s. She is the author of *Proud Shoes: The Story of an American Family* (1978) and *Dark Testament* (1970). Murray's awards include the Whitney M. Young, Jr., Memorial Award and the Robert F. Kennedy Book Award. She has also been inducted into Hunter College's Hall of Fame.

Gordon Nelson (1953-) was born in Bronx, New York. Nelson is a poet and playwright. Nelson's play *The Legacy: Memories of Gospel Song* was produced at the National Black Theater. Nelson currently lives in Mt. Vernon, New York.

Abiodun Oyewole (1948-) is a founding member of the famed Last Poets, the precursors of contemporary rap music. Oyewole was raised primarily in New York and began writing as a child. Oyewole is strongly connected to the African American oral tradition and frequently presents his poetry throughout the country. Oyewole is a playwright and teacher. He is the leading member of a jazz band called Griot, meaning "African Storyteller."

Jean Parrish is a poet whose poetry remains vital and in print. Additional information about Ms. Parrish is unavailable.

Conrad Kent Rivers (1933-1968) was born in Atlantic City, New Jersey. He was educated at Chicago Teachers College and Indiana University. Rivers was the author of *Perchance to Dream* (1959), *These Black Bodies and This Sun-Burnt Face* (1962), *Dusk At Selma* (1965) and *The Still Voice of Harlem* (1968). Rivers was a founding member of the Chicago-based literary group called

Organization of Black American Culture. Rivers was a widely anthologized writer who constantly questioned the role of the African American writer in the United States.

Sonia Sanchez (1935-) was born in Birmingham, Alabama. Sanchez is a poet, playwright, professor and activist. She is the author of *Homecoming*, *We a baddDDD People*, *It's a New Day*, and *Homegirls and Handgrenades*. Sanchez's poetry is reflective of the 1960s street poetry and free verse. Sanchez is a fiery and impressive orator. She is the former wife of poet Etheridge Knight and is the mother of three children. She currently teaches at Temple University in Pennsylvania. In 1992, she was awarded the African Poetry Theatre Award for Excellence in Poetry.

Gil Scott-Heron (1949-) was born in Chicago, Illinois. Scott-Heron is a musician, poet, composer, pianist, vocalist, teacher, and lyricist. He was raised in Jacksonville, Tennessee, and attended Lincoln University and Johns Hopkins University. Heron is known for his music, but he is also an accomplished writer and poet. He is the author of *Small Talk at One Hundred Twenty-Fifth and Lenox* (1970), *The Vulture* (1970) and *The Nigger Factory* (1972). His awards include the Langston Hughes Creative Writing Award and a host of musical awards. Heron is known for his political and streetwise poetry.

Ntozake Shange (formerly Paulette Williams) (1947-) is a poet, playwright, novelist, professor, and lecturer. She was born in Trenton, New Jersey and attended Barnard College and the University of California in Los Angeles. The translation of Shange's Zulu name is "she who owns her own things" and "she who walks like a lion." Shange is best known for her "choreopoem" *For Colored Girls Who Have Considered Suicide When the Rainbow is Enuf* (1976), for which she received a Tony Award. Shange is also the author of *Nappy Edges* (1978), *Sassafrass, Indigo and Cypress* (1982) and *Betsy Brown*.

Joyce Carol Thomas (1938-) was born in Ponca City, Oklahoma. She is the mother of four and currently lives in Knoxville, Tennessee. She is a graduate of San Jose State College and Stanford University and is fluent in Spanish. She is an award-winning author of several books for children. Thomas's most popular books are: *Marked by Fire* (1982), *Bright Shadow* (1983), *Water Girl* (1986) and *Black Child Inside the*

Rainbow. She has been awarded the American Book Award for Children's Books (1983), the Before Columbus Award, and the Coretta Scott King Award (1984). In 1982, *Marked by Fire* was voted the Outstanding Book of the Year by the American Library Association and The New York Times.

Alice Walker (1944-) is a writer, poet, essayist, professor, and activist. Walker was born in 1944 in Eatonton, Georgia. She attended Spelman College and graduated from Sarah Lawrence University. Walker is the co-founder and publisher of Wild Trees Press. She is the author of *Once, Revolutionary Petunia, Goodnight, Willie Lee, I'll See You in the Morning*, and *Meridian* (1976). *The Color Purple* is perhaps her most well-known work. In 1983 she received the Pulitzer Prize and the National Book Award for *The Color Purple*. She has also been the recipient of a National Endowment Grant for the Arts, the Guggenheim Award, and a National Book Critics Circle Award nomination. Walker is known for her authentic rendering of African American life and her feminist philosophy.

Margaret Abigail Walker (1915-) came to critical acclaim with her first book of poetry, *For My People*, which earned her the Yale Younger Award in 1942. Walker was born in Birmingham, Alabama, and was raised in New Orleans and Mississippi. Walker, who has been writing poetry since she was thirteen, was educated at Northwestern University and Iowa State College. Walker taught at Jackson State University in Jackson, Mississippi from 1949 until 1979. She has been a Rosenwald Fellow, and in 1966, received the Houghton Mifflin Fellowship for her novel, *Jubilee*. Her recent works include: *Prophets for a New Day*, (1970), *The Daemonic Genius of Richard Wright* (1987) and *This is My Century* (1989). Walker is a master of form and feeling. The poem "Lineage" first appeared in *For My People*.

GLOSSARY

A

abhor (ab-HOR) hate (5)

abhorrence (ab-HOR-rens) hatred (31)

Abrams, General Creighton W. (1914–1974) commanding general of the U.S. forces in Vietnam from 1968 to 1972 (48)

absence (AB-sens) lack (28)

adversaries (AD-ver-sair-eez) enemies (32)

adversities (ad-VER-su-teez) difficulties; challenges (32)

Agnew, Spiro (1918–) U.S. vice president under President Nixon who resigned in 1973 after a history of political corruption (48)

Ali, Muhammad (formerly Cassius Clay) (1942–) heavyweight world champion boxer; considered to be the all-time greatest boxer (67)

Ali, Noble Drew (formerly Timothy Drew) (1886–?) religious leader and founder of the Moorish Science Temple of America (42)

ambitions (am-BISH-uhnz) goals very strongly desired (11)

ancestors (AN-ses-terz) people from whom one is descended; parents, grandparents, and so on (13)

ancient (AYN-shunt) very old (66)

Anderson, Marian (1902–) singer considered to be one of the world's greatest contraltos; first African American opera singer admitted to New York's Metropolitan Opera Company (67)

armor (AHR-mer) a protective covering (32)

assignments (uh-SEYEN-ments) tasks one is asked or required to perform (40)

attain (uh-TAYN) gain, achieve (43)

aura (AWR-uh) a self-generated glow that seems to surround a person or thing (78)

austere (aw-STAIR) strict; stern (76)

B

ban (BAN) forbid by official order (8)

barren (BAIR-en) unproductive (22)

battered (BAT-erd) hit over and over; pounded (35)

belligerence (buh-LIHJ-uh-rens) hostility or anger (41)

beset (bih-SET) surrounded (12)

Bethune, Mary McLeod (1875–1955) educator and advisor to presidents Herbert Hoover and Franklin D. Roosevelt; founder of

Bethune-Cookman College in Florida (67)

"Beverly Hillbillies" popular television situation comedy of the 1960s and 1970s (50)

biased (BEYE-uhsd) unfair (32)

Black Panthers grassroots political-activist party of the 1960s and 1970s (42)

blues (BLYOOZ) African American folk music with a slow tempo and sad words (67)

bolstered (BOHL-sterd) supported (58)

booby-trapped (BOO-bee-trapt) containing hidden traps or bombs with trick triggers (35)

bough (BOW) a large branch of a tree (6)

Brooke, Edward W. (1919–) U.S. senator from Massachusetts in 1966; first African American to be elected to the U.S. senate in the twentieth century (67)

Brooks, Gwendolyn (1917–) first African American to win a Pulitzer Prize for poetry (53)

Bullwinkle (BULL-weenk-uhl) popular cartoon moose of the late 1960s (48)

bunion (BUN-yun) swelling at the bottom of the big toe (71)

C

Cadillacs (CAD-uh-laks) expensive American-made cars; status symbols (31)

Campbell, Glen popular country and western musician of the 1970s (50)

capitalism (KAP-ih-tuhl-IZ-uhm) a system where money and other resources are attained for private profit rather than being controlled by a state or government (39)

captive (KAP-tiv) prisoner (31)

Cash, Johnny popular country and western singer and songwriter, particularly in the 1970s (50)

cast (KAST) to cause to fall upon or over something (26)

catapulted (KAT-uh-pool-ted) sprung, as if from a slingshot (14)

celebrate (SEL-uh-brayt) honor, particularly with a public ritual (66)

chalice (CHAL-ihs) a cup; goblet (6)

chastening (CHAST-ning) punishing; disciplining (25)

chronic (KRAHN-ik) lasting for a long time (76)

cinders (SIHN-derz) ashes from wood or coal (14)

Cinque (SIN-kyoo), **Joseph** (circa 1811–1878) African who led a revolt aboard the slave ship *L'Amistad* in 1839 (42)

clenched (KLENCHD) gripped tightly (46) (23)

Coke refers to ad slogan used by Coca Cola to sell their soda (50)

confiscated (KAHN-fihs-kay-tihd) took or seized (48)
contralto (kahn-TRAL-toh) the lowest female singing voice (55)
cooperation (koh-ahp-uh-RAY-shun) joint effort (40)
copped (KAHPT) got or received (56)
courted (KOR-tihd) risked (42)
coveted (KUHV-uh-tihd) highly desired (53)
curse (KERS) a profane word or phrase often used in anger (2)
cynical (SIHN-ih-kuhl) sarcastic (41)

D

dead run (DED RUN) the act of running as fast as one can (48)
deemed (DEEMD) judged to be; considered (55)
defy (dih-FEYE) to resist, challenge (79)
denounced (dih-NOWNST) condemned (11)
deride (dee-REYED) laugh at; scorn (5)
despair (dihs-PAIR) to be without hope (21)
destinations (des-tih-NAY-shunz) the places to which an object or person is going (5) (66)
destiny (DEST-uh-nee) fate (52)
ditty (DIHT-ee) a simple song (23)
doughboy (DOH-BOI) the name for a U.S. soldier who fought in World War I (77)
Douglass, Frederick (1817–1895) escaped enslaved African American author, orator, and abolitionist (42)
drum in your bedroom refers to a television ad of the 1970s for a popular cleanser (50)
Du Bois (doo-BOIZ), **W.E.B.** (1868–1895) educator, scholar, author, and civil rights leader (42)
Dumas (DOO-mahs), **Alexander** French author of African ancestry; *The Three Musketeers* is perhaps his best-known book (67)

E

ebony (EB-uh-nee) black in color, like ebony wood (67)
ecstasy (EK-stuh-see) joy; delight (14)
ego (EE-goh) the self; one's awareness about oneself (41)
elemental (el-uh-MEN-tuhl) relating to the forces of nature (36)
emancipation (ee-MAN-sih-PAY-shun) freedom from bonds or slavery (10)
encircled (ihn-SER-kuhld) formed a circle around; surrounded (75)
endeavors (en-DEV-erz) earnest efforts (40)
endure (ihn-DYOOR) stand pain or suffering; tolerate (9)

Evers, Medgar (1925–1963) assassinated civil rights activist; president of the Jackson, Mississippi NAACP in 1963 (42)

F
fain (FAYN) gladly; willingly (6)

fertile (FER-tuhl) able to produce abundantly (18)

folkways (FOHK-WAYZ) the practices or beliefs of a people or social group (40)

forefathers (FOR-fah-therz) ancestors (40)

frailties (FRAYL-teez) weaknesses (30)

fruit of my womb child; offspring (21)

G
Garvey, Marcus (1887–1940) African American nationalist in the 1920s; founder of the Negro Improvement Association (42)

garveyite (gahr-VEE-eyet) a follower of Marcus Garvey (77)

germs that may cause bad breath refers to an ad slogan for mouthwash (50)

giant in your toilet bowl refers to a television ad of the 1970s for a popular cleanser (50)

gleam (GLEEM) a ray or beam of light (26)

gloriously (GLOR-ee-uhs-lee) beautifully (36)

glum (GLUM) gloomy and silent (21)

"Green Acres" popular television show of the 1970s (50)

H
Hampton Institute located in Hampton, Virginia; one of the first institutions of higher learning for African Americans (66)

harassed (huh-RAST or HAIR-ihst) bothered over and over again (41)

Harper's Ferry Raid attack on the federal arsenal at Harper's Ferry (West Virginia), led by John Brown in 1859 (42)

haughtiness (HAW-tee-nes) pride in oneself and scorn for others (12)

headragged (HED-ragd) wearing rags around the head (35)

headstone (HED-STOHN) the stone placed at the head of a grave (68)

heritage (HER-uh-tihj) elements of culture handed down from one generation to the next (40)

hog mauls (MAWLZ) traditional southern food made from the jowls of the hog (48)

Holiday, Billie (1915–1959) jazz and blues singer; often called "Lady Day" (67)

homage (AH-mihj) honor; respect (56)

"Hooterville Junction" refers to "Petticoat Junction," a popular television show of the 1960s and 1970s (50)

Hoover, Herbert (1874–1964) president of the United States from 1929 to 1933 (80)

hopscotch (HOP-skoch) children's game where players hop between squares drawn on the sidewalk (2)

hue (HYOO) color, or shade of a color (78) (79)

Hughes, Langston (1902–1967) outstanding poet, often called the "Negro poet laureate" (67)

Hughes's blues refers to African American writer Langston Hughes, who combined blues music with his poetry (67)

Humperdinck, Englebert a popular singer of the 1970s (50)

hurtling (HERT-ling) moving quickly and with great force (15)

husky (HUHS-kee) sounding deep and hoarse (35)

I

iced (EYEST) killed (43)

indifferently (ihn-DIHF-er-uhnt-lee) in an unconcerned or uncaring way (76)

inhuman (ihn-HYOO-muhn) cruel, brutal, or monstrous (32)

initiative (ih-NISH-ee-uh-tihv) energy and desire to begin or to move forward (40)

institute, the refers to Tuskegee Institute in Tuskegee, Alabama (71)

instruments (IHN-stroo-ments) objects for producing musical sounds (8)

insurmountable (ihn-ser-MOWN-tih-buhl) impossible to overcome (43)

intricacies (IHN-trih-kuh-seez) details that are often complicated and involved (59)

irresponsible (ir-rih-SPAHN-sih-buhl) not reliable; not thinking about the outcome of one's actions (40)

J

javelin (JAV-uh-lihn) spear (69)

Jones, Tom a popular singer, particularly in the 1970s (50)

Julia refers to the popular television show of the late 1960s starring Diahann Carroll; one of first primetime shows to star an African American (48)

justice (JUHS-tihs) fairness; a figure representing fairness (5)

K

keener (KEEN-er) sharper (6)

kegged (KEGD) put in barrels (9)

Key, Francis Scott (1779-1843) lawyer, poet, and author of the national anthem, "The Star-Spangled Banner" (50)

King, Martin Luther, Jr. (1929–1968) assassinated Baptist minister and leader of the Southern Christian Leadership Conference (SCLC); activist for African American and poor people's civil rights (42)

L

laid (LAYD) slang for looking good; attractively dressed (74)
languorous (LAYNG-uh-ruhs) lacking in interest or spirit (10)
lashed (LASHT) whipped (5)
liberationists (lihb-uh-RAY-shun-ists) supporters of women's liberation, a movement begun in the 1970s which sought to give women more choice about their role in society (50)
Lincoln University founded in 1854 and located in Oxford, Pennsylvania, the first African American college in the United States; originally called Ashmum Institute (66)
lineage (LIHN-ee-ihj) family history, ancestry (27)
loom (LOOM) to appear unclearly, but seemingly large and frightful (5)
loon (LOON) a web-footed diving bird (20)
luminous (LOO-mih-nuhs) giving off light (79)
lurched (LERCHT) moved suddenly (14)

M

mahogany (muh-HAHG-uh-nee) a reddish-brown hardwood (78)
Malcolm X (Al Hajj Malik Al-Shabazz) (1925–1965) assassinated Muslim minister and activist for African American and human rights (69)
Marshall, Thurgood (1908–) first African American U.S. Supreme Court Justice; served from 1967 to 1991 (67)
Mays, Willie (1931–) outstanding baseball player who, in the history of the game, ranks third highest in the number of career home runs (48)
McQueen, Steve popular actor of the 1960s and 1970s (48)
meager (MEE-ger) small (20)
mined (MEYEND) filled with hidden bombs (35)
Mitchell, John (1913–1988) U.S. attorney general under President Nixon; Nixon's campaign manager in 1972 and during the Watergate break-in (48)
mocha (MOH-kuh) a choice coffee originally from Arabia (79)

N

nappy (NAP-ee) **headed** having short, usually uncombed hair (31)
NBC...29 districts refers to predictions television networks make about election winners (48)
Nile (NEYEL) a river in northern Africa (32)
Nixon, Richard M. (1913–) U.S. president who resigned in 1974 after

the Watergate break-in was uncovered (48)
noble (NOH-buhl) highly moral (42)
nubs (NUBZ) slang for whiskers (48)

O

obscured (ahb-SKYOORD) not easily seen; hidden (32)
obstacles (AHB-stih-kuhlz) things which stand in the way (11)
offspring (AHF-SPRING) the young of a person, animal, or plant (43)
omitted (oh-MIHT-tihd) left out (32)
Onassis (oh-NAS-ihs), **Jackie** widow of President John F. Kennedy who
    later married wealthy Greek businessman Aristotle Onassis (50)
opes (OHPS) opens (6)
oppression (uh-PRESH-uhn) the act of being pushed or held down
mentally and physically (42)
oppressors (oh-PRES-erz) people who unfairly keep down others (9)
Owens, Jessie (1913–1980) track runner who, in the 1936 Berlin
    Olympic games, won four gold medals (67)

P

perch (PERCH) a place used for sitting or standing upon (6)
petunia (pih-TOON-yuh) colorful flower (36)
portraits (POR-trihts) pictures of people, especially their faces (66)
potent (POHT-ihnt) powerful (9)
potentially (poh-TEN-chuhl-ee) possibly (44)
preoccupied (pree-AHK-yoo-peyed) fully interested in (41)
prevail (prih-VAYL) succeed; dominate (30) (11)
process (PRAH-ses) chemical treatment to straighten hair (49) (44)
profound (pruh-FOWND) intense (78)
projection (proh-JEK-shuhn) that which has moved forward or
    outward (41)
prone (PROHN) naturally leaning or tending (40)
propriety (pruh-PREYE-uh-tee) proper or fitting behavior (77)
Prosser, Gabriel (circa 1776–1800) organizer of an unsuccessful slave
    uprising in Richmond, Virginia in 1800 (42)
Pushkin, Aleksandr (1799–1837) Russian poet of African ancestry (67)
pyramids (PEER-uh-midz) tombs for Egyptian kings (66)

R

R., Harry refers to Harry Reasoner, network newscaster in the
    1970s and 1980s (50)
race (RAYS) groups within all humanity that share the same ancestors (14)
rap (RAP) slang for talk; popular music of the 1980s and 1990s where

words are spoken rather than sung (44)

Rare Earth a popular rock group of the 1970s (50)

rared (RAIRD) a variation of the word reared, meaning "raised up" (10)

reap (REEP) gather the results of one's planting (5)

rebellious (rih-BEL-yus) resisting control (36)

relevant (REL-uh-vihnt) current (50)

resound (rih-ZOWND) to be filled with sound; to echo back (25)

revolution (rev-uh-LOO-shun) major change in government or social order (44) (48)

revolutionary (rev-uh-LOO-shun-air-ee) facing great odds to grow or bring about change (39) (44)

rhetoric (RET-awr-ihk) artful use of words, written and spoken (39)

ridiculed (RIHD-ih-kyoold) made fun of (11)

Robeson, Paul (1898–1976) reknowned athlete, singer, actor and scholar (67)

S

sable (SAY-buhl) black or dark brown in color (32)

sacrifice (SAK-rih-feyes) give up (32)

sanctuary (SANK-choo-wair-ee) a holy place (48)

sassiness (SAS-ee-nes) sauciness; bold talk (12)

Schaefer (SHAY-fer) **Award Theatre** also known as Schaefer Century Theatre; television show of the early 1950s (48)

scufflin (SKUHF-lihn) scuffling; fighting roughly (80)

sculptor (SKULP-ter) artist who creates images from wood, clay, stone, or metal (52)

"Search for Tomorrow" popular soap opera (50)

semantics (suh-MAN-tihks) the many ways in which one can express the same idea (41)

serene (suh-REEN) calm; peaceful; untroubled (32) (79)

sinews (SIN-yooz) tendons (14)

slew (SLYOO) a large number (56)

slumped (SLUMPT) hung loosely; drooped (70)

soliloquy (suh-LIHL-uh-kwee) method used in drama where characters reveal their inner thoughts to the audience by speaking out loud (52)

sorority (suh-RAWR-ih-tee) all-female social, political or professional organization; usually identified by one or more Greek letters (58)

SOS (ES-oh-ES) a call for help, originally used as a code by telegraph operators (38)

soul (SOHL) person; being (28)

soulful (SOHL-fuhl) full of deep feeling (12)

sowing (SOH-ing) planting seeds or ideas for growing (5)

spikes (SPEYEKS) metal points on the bottom of athletic shoes (14)

sprawlingly (SPRAWL-ing-lee) in an awkward, ungraceful way (10)

starched (STARCHT) stiffened with a special laundry powder (35)

statistics (stuh-TIHS-tiks) numerical facts gathered to support an idea (40)

statues (STACH-ooz) models of persons or animals, often to honor their importance (8)

stout (STOWT) strong; determined (35)

straight (STRAYT) following a fixed pattern (80)

straightaway (STRAYT-uh-way) straight part of a race track (15)

streaks (STREEKS) uneven stripes (29)

stretch (STRECH) the final part of a race (14)

sturdiness (STER-dee-nes) strength (27)

subtle (SUT-uhl) not direct or obvious (19)

T

televised (TEL-uh-veyezd) shown on television (48)

tiger in your tank refers to a television ad of the 1970s for a popular gasoline product (50)

Timbuktu (tihm-buhk-TOO) city located in Ghana, Africa; home of the world-reknowned University of Sankore (66)

toil (TOYL) to work hard (27)

treading (TRED-ing) walking or stepping on (25)

trends (TREHNDZ) general courses or directions; fads (40)

triumphant (treye-UM-fuhnt) successful (14)

trod (TRAHD) walk or step on (12)

Truth, Sojourner (1797–1883) preacher, abolitionist, and lecturer (42)

Tubman, Harriet (1820?–1913) escaped enslaved African American who became the most famous conductor of the underground railroad (52)

Turner, Nat (1800-1831) enslaved African American who, in 1831, led a slave rebellion in Virginia (40)

Tuskegee (tus-KEE-gee) **Institute** University for African Americans located in Tuskegee, Alabama; founded by Booker T. Washington in 1881 (66)

twilight (TWEYE-leyet) time after sunset before it is completely dark (9)

U

unconventional (un-kun-VEN-chuhn-uhl) not going along with the usual, accepted ways or rules (40)

undaunted (un-DAWNT-ihd) not discouraged or fearful (40)

unstilled (un-STIHLD) not kept still; allowed or helped to move (40)

unwarped (un-WORPT) not twisted; whole (32)

upland (UP-land) the higher part of a region (6)

urgent (ER-jent) very important (38)

V

Vesey (VEE-zee), **Denmark** (1767?–1822) African American who, in 1822, led an elaborate conspiracy to take over Charleston, South Carolina (42)

venerate (VEN-er-ayt) honor; respect (33)

villains (VIL-uhnz) wicked characters (31)

vow (VOW) promise (5)

W

Washington, Booker T. (1856–1915) educator and founder of Tuskegee Institute (66)

Watts (WAHTS) South Central Los Angeles, California; location of the 1965 race riot (49)

weary (WEER-ee) tired; fatigued (25)

Webb, Jim popular singer and songwriter of the 1960s and 1970s (50)

welling (WEL-ing) pouring out; overflowing (13)

white tornado refers to a television ad of the 1970s for a popular cleanser (50)

Wilkins, Roy (1901–1981) executive secretary of the National Association for the Advancement of Colored People (NAACP) during the1960s (49)

wondrously (WUN-druhs-lee) wonderfully (13)

Wood, Natalie popular actress during the late 1950s, 1960s, and early 1970s (49)

Wright, Richard (1908–1960) best-selling author of novels and short stories (67)

X

Xerox (ZEER-ahks) major company which produces and sells business machines (48)

Y

yearning (YERN-ing) deep longing; an earnest desire (9)

yielded (YEELD-ihd) gave forth; produced (20)

Young, Whitney M., Jr. (1921–1971) executive director of the National Urban League in the 1960s (49)

Z

Zimbabwe (zim-BAHB-way) a country in Southern Africa; formerly called Southern Rhodesia (66)

INDEX OF POETS

ACKNOWLEDGMENTS

Globe Book Company wishes to thank the following copyright owners for permission to reproduce poetry in this book:

AFRICA WORLD PRESS, for John Henrik Clarke, "Encouragement II" and "Love" from *The Early Poems of John Henrik Clarke*. Originally published by Decker Press, 1948. First Africa World Edition 1991. Copyright © 1991 John Henrik Clarke. / Suliaman El Hadi, "Blessed Are Those Who Struggle" from *The Last Poets: Vibes From the Scribes*. Copyright © 1992 Jalal Nuriddin and Suliaman El Hadi. / Ja A. Jahannes, "Being Black in My Neighborhood" and "If We Forget" from *Truthfeasting*. Copyright © 1990 Ja A. Jahannes. All rights reserved. **MARGARET WALKER ALEXANDER,** for Margaret Walker, "Lineage" from *This Is My Century, New and Collected Poems by Margaret Walker*. Published by University of Georgia Press, 1989. Copyright 1947 by Margaret Walker Alexander. **DESIRÉE BARNWELL,** for "Will the Real Black People Please Stand," from *Night Comes Softly*, edited by Nikki Giovanni, William Morrow and Company, 1970. Reprinted by permission of Desirée Barnwell. **BIENSTOCK PUBLISHING COMPANY,** for Gil Scott-Heron, "The Revolution Will Not Be Televised" from *The Revolution Will Not Be Televised*. © 1978 Bienstock Publishing Company. All rights reserved. **BOA EDITIONS, LTD.,** 92 Park Avenue, Brockport, New York 14420: Lucille Clifton, "the lesson of the falling leaves" from *good woman: poems and a memoir 1969-1980*. Copyright © 1987 by Lucille Clifton. All rights reserved. **DENISE BROOKS,** 1313 Baltimore Avenue, Linden, New Jersey 07036, for Denise Brooks, "Variety in Black." Copyright, 1984 Denise Sanders Brooks. **GWENDOLYN BROOKS,** for Gwendolyn Brooks, "Speech to the Young/Speech to the Progress-Toward" from *Blacks*. © 1987 Gwendolyn Brooks. Re-issued by Third World Press, Chicago, 1991. © 1991 Gwendolyn Brooks. **MARGARET BURROUGHS,** for "What Shall I Tell My Children Who Are Black," from *Night Comes Softly*, edited by Nikki Giovanni, William Narrow & Company, 1970. Copyright © Margaret Burroughs. Reprinted by permission of Margaret Burroughs. **PHYLLIS BYNUM,** for Phyllis Bynum, "Our Promise." © 1989 TXV 3 57 463, Phyllis M. Bynum. **FRANCES COLLIN,** Literary Agent, for Pauli Murray, "#8" in "Dark Testament" and "To the Oppressors" from *Dark Testament and Other Poems*. Copyright © 1970 Pauli Murray. **HARDY CROSSLIN,** for Hardy Crosslin, "We are..." from *Regeneration: Poems by Hardy Crosslin*. Published by John Colton Associates, Atlanta. Copyright © 1982 by Hardy Crosslin. Every effort has been made to contact Hardy Crosslin. The publishers would be very interested to hear from the copyright owner. **JAMES A. EMANUEL,** for James A. Emanuel, "For Malcolm, U.S.A." from *Whole Grain: Collected Poems, 1958-1989*. Published by Lotus Press, Detroit, 1991. **MARI E. EVANS,** for Mari E. Evans, "The Emancipation of George-Hector (a colored turtle)." **HARCOURT BRACE JOVANOVICH, INC.,** for "The Nature of This Flower Is to Bloom" from *Revolutionary Petunias and Other Poems*, copyright © 1973 by Alice Walker, and for "Women" from *Revolutionary Petunias and Other Poems*, copyright © 1970 by Alice Walker, both reprinted by permission of Harcourt Brace Jovanovich, Inc. **HAROLD OBER ASSOCIATES, INC.,** for Arna Bontemps, "A Note of Humility" from *Personals*. Copyright © 1963 by Arna Bontemps. **HIRT MUSIC, INC.,** c/o Purcell Associates, New York, New York: Maya Angelou, "Harlem Hopscotch." **FRANK SMITH HORNE** for Frank Smith Horne, "To James" in "Letters Found Near a Suicide" from *In Haverstraw*. Published by Paul Breman, London, 1963. Copyright © 1963 by Frank Horne. Reprinted in *American Negro Poetry* edited by Arna Bontemps, copyright © 1974 by The Estate of Arna Bontemps. Every effort has been made to contact Frank Horne's estate. The publishers would be very interested to hear from the copyright owner.